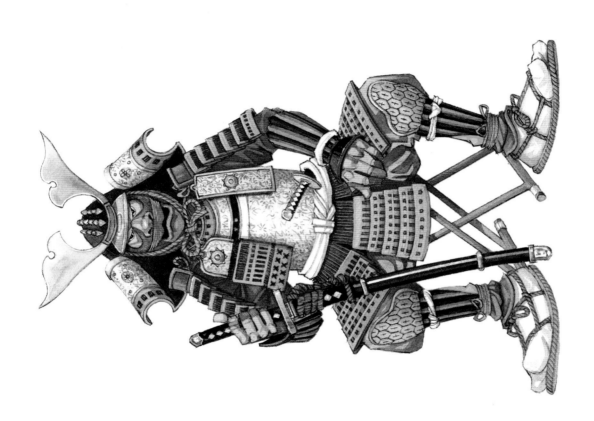

Author:
Fiona Macdonald studied history at Cambridge University and the University of East Anglia, both in England. She has taught in schools and universities and is the author of numerous books for children on historical topics.

Artist:
David Antram was born in Brighton, England, in 1958. He studied at Eastbourne College of Art and then worked in advertising for fifteen years before becoming a full-time artist. He has illustrated many children's nonfiction books.

Series creator:
David Salariya was born in Dundee, Scotland. He has illustrated a wide range of books and has created and designed many new series for publishers in the UK and overseas. In 1989 he established The Salariya Book Company. He lives in Brighton with his wife, illustrator Shirley Willis, and their son Jonathan.

Editor: **Tanya Kant**

Editorial Assistant: **Mark Williams**

© The Salariya Book Company Ltd MMIX

No part of this publication may be reproduced in whole or in part, or stored in a retrieval system, or transmitted in any form or by any means, electronic, mechanical, photocopying, recording, or otherwise, without written permission of the publisher. For information regarding permission, write to the copyright holder.

Published in Great Britain in 2009 by
The Salariya Book Company Ltd
25 Marlborough Place, Brighton BN1 1UB

ISBN-13: 978-0-531-21325-4 (lib. bdg.)   978-0-531-20516-7 (pbk.)
ISBN-10: 0-531-21325-0 (lib. bdg.)   0-531-20516-9 (pbk.)

A CIP catalog record for this book is available from the Library of Congress.

Printed and bound in China.
Printed on paper from sustainable sources.

SCHOLASTIC, FRANKLIN WATTS, and associated logos are trademarks and/or registered trademarks of Scholastic Inc.

You Wouldn't Want to Be a Samurai!

Written by
Fiona Macdonald

Illustrated by
David Antram

Created and designed by
David Salariya

A Deadly Career You'd Rather Not Pursue

Franklin Watts®

An Imprint of Scholastic Inc.

NEW YORK   TORONTO   LONDON   AUCKLAND   SYDNEY

MEXICO CITY   NEW DELHI   HONG KONG

DANBURY, CONNECTICUT

Contents

Introduction

Well, here we are! The place? Japan. The time? The early 17th century. And you—you're a young boy from an ordinary Japanese family. Like other boys, you've seen noble *samurai* warriors marching off to war. And you've heard wonderful stories about samurai heroes who have won brave battles, performed amazing feats of swordsmanship, survived countless adventures—and even had magical powers!

You'd like to be a samurai when you grow up—and astonish everyone with your courage and skill. But a samurai's life isn't just glamorous and exciting; it's also hard and dangerous. For centuries, samurai have been fighting among themselves for wealth and power. There are new laws designed to stop samurai wars, but these laws also prevent ordinary boys like you from becoming warriors. Perhaps that's not so bad! Read this book, think carefully, and then ask yourself: "Would I really want to be a samurai?"

Japanese Society

JAPAN has an ancient, traditional society. Everyone knows their place and must show respect to their superiors. It is extremely difficult to move up in social rank.

Emperor and royal family

Shogun (top army commander)

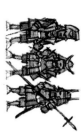

Daimyo *(ancient noble lords): they own estates and castles, and some lead armies.*

Warlords: *they lead armies and have won power through battle.*

Ashigaru *(ordinary soldiers) and samurai*

Farmers *and their families*

Merchants, *craftspeople, and townspeople*

Buddhist *holy teachers, monks, and nuns. Their rank depends on their family.*

Not for You!

Samurai first became famous around AD 1200. At that time, any brave fighting man could apply to join a warlord's army as a samurai ("man who serves"). But in 1590, General Toyotomi Hideyoshi took control of Japan. He banned everyone except the samurai of that time—and their sons—from owning or fighting with swords. Nowadays, samurai can be recruited only from old samurai families, not from ordinary families like yours. So you're out of luck!

Who Can't Be a Samurai?

FARMERS are needed at home. They grow the food that keeps all Japanese people alive.

ENTERTAINERS. Funny, tragic, dramatic—these people are talented! But they are not welcome in respectable society.

Emperor

Shogun

Samurai

Handy Hint

Unfortunately, you can't fight if you're left-handed! You might get in the way of your comrades, who all hold their swords in their right hands.

But don't be sad! You're not alone. Most people in Japan cannot be samurai, no matter how much they admire samurai courage, dedication, and skill. Samurai are elite, expert warriors. They share a proud history of war service that goes back hundreds of years.

WOMEN AND GIRLS. Traditionally, Japanese people have believed that fighting is a task for men. There have been a few women warriors, but they are rare exceptions!

THE EMPEROR is the most honored man in Japan, but the shogun is the most powerful. Since 1192, shoguns have ruled Japan on behalf of the emperors. *Shogun* means "great general."

MOST JAPANESE distrust foreigners. In the late 1200s, Mongol warriors from the Asian mainland tried to invade Japan. Recently, new strangers have arrived—Christian missionaries from Europe.

Tough Training

Training to be a samurai begins when pupils are very young—at about the age of seven. And the training is very tough. It aims to turn the most timid youngsters into powerful warriors by teaching them all sorts of fighting techniques and survival skills. As a student, you'd spend years learning how to handle weapons. You'd also study reading, history, poetry, and handwriting.

Your training would shape your character as well: a samurai must have good manners, respect for others, and self-discipline. And you'd be taught to live—or die—for your comrades, as a loyal member of a team. Could you spend your childhood training this way? Or would you rather live peacefully at home with your friends and family?

BE BRAVE! Battle practice can be terrifying—and very painful. But pupils soon learn to defend themselves and fight back.

SCHOOL will train a pupil's mind. Samurai families admire scholarship and knowledge.

READING AND WRITING are useful skills. They are also signs of a noble, gracious person.

On second thought, I think I'll be a farmer!

But when do I get to fight?

The pen and the sword in accord. *

* Old Japanese phrase. It means "Learning and fighting are equally important."

Handy Hint

Be lucky! If you have bad luck or have not studied hard, you might die in your first battle.

Ready to Graduate

WHEN PUPILS are about 14 years old, they take part in a *genbuku* coming-of-age ceremony and will be allowed to tie up their hair in the special samurai style. Now they are ready to fight!

PUPILS are taught to honor their teachers and fighting masters. These teachers are very wise—and worth listening to.

STUDY STRATEGY by playing traditional board games such as *go*. These games will teach a pupil to think ahead and outwit his enemies.

PUPILS LISTEN to stories about famous samurai who lived long ago. Their glorious adventures inspire everyone!

A Special Sword

Samurai fight with several different weapons: spears for thrusting and stabbing, bows that shoot deadly arrows, and newly invented guns that fire metal balls. But a samurai's most important weapon—and his most treasured possession—is his long, sharp sword. The best swords have such fine, flexible blades that some people say they are alive!

Samurai like to have as many swords as possible. They can buy them (though swords are very expensive), inherit them from their fathers, capture them from dead enemies, or receive them as rewards for bravery. Wearing a sword is a sign of wealth, skill, and high rank. So if you see a swordsman, be respectful.

THE BEST SWORDS are made by expert craftsmen, who can hammer, twist, and fold iron into secret patterns. There are several sword designs. A samurai wears his *katana* sword (shown at right) with the sharp edge up.

SWORD FIGHTING. It takes a lifetime of training to master fighting with a samurai sword. First, bow to your teacher, fighting partner—or enemy!

A samurai always sleeps with his sword by his side. *

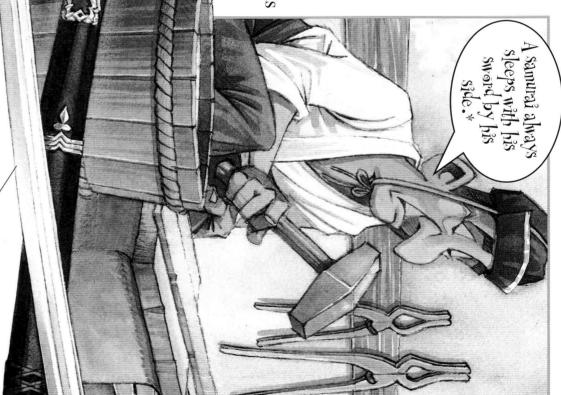

*An old Japanese saying

Sharp edge

Handy Hint

Watch your fingers! Fit a *tsuba* (circular guard) to your sword-blade, to keep from slicing your hand.

Tsuba

THEN, draw your sword. Now you must try to do two things at once: attack your opponent and guard yourself against his attack.

IT'S NOT EASY! Sooner or later, one of you will get your sword close enough to strike a winning blow. Will you be victorious?

Magic Weapons

TALL TAIL? There are many amazing stories about samurai warriors and their swords. Famous, fearless Prince Yamato, who lived around 110 BC, was said to fight with a sword that was found in a magic serpent's tail!

That looks sharp!

Katana sword

Awkward Armor

Do you know how you'd survive a battle if you were a samurai? You'd need skillful swordsmanship, bravery, and luck. But, just as important, you'd need armor!

Samurai protect their heads with helmets and their bodies with elaborate suits of metal. Their chests and backs are shielded by rigid iron plates, laced or riveted together. A samurai's arms and thighs are covered with chain mail or panels of tough rawhide. All this armor is hot, stiff, and weighs 40 pounds (18 kg)!

SAMURAI ARMOR makes running or jumping difficult, and you'd need help taking it off and putting it on.

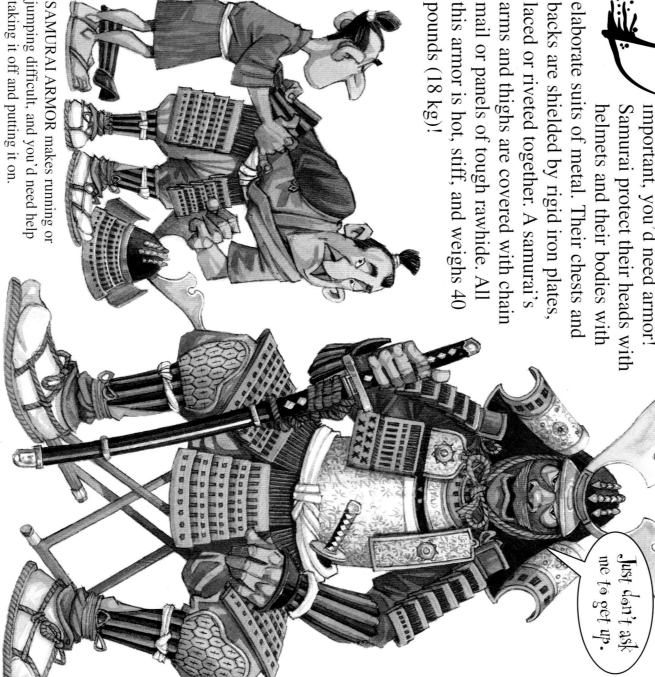

Just don't ask me to get up.

Handy Hint

Stand far back! Modern guns, introduced from Europe soon after AD 1542, can shoot very far and very fast.

Lower Ranks, Less Protection

ASHIGARU (ordinary soldiers) wear armor made of thin, light-weight strips of metal. It's better than nothing, but it's a poor defense against swords, arrows, or bullets!

Metal bullets? That's not fair!

YOUR HELMET should be a work of art, made of 32 separate pieces. Could you afford to have one made?

YOUR ANGRY FACE-MASK should look fearsome—but it's hard to see while wearing one.

YOUR SURCOAT (cloth overcoat) must be splendid and must display your family badge —a symbol that represents your family. But it's a tight fit over all of that armor—this might make walking difficult!

THE CREST on top of your helmet will stick up high— beware of low-hanging objects!

Thunk!

Could You Hop onto a Horse?

For honor!

For glory!

Traditionally, Japanese people have always fought on foot. Now, samurai ride on horses. They rely on horses to charge into battle or to carry them through enemy territory. Horses are much stronger and faster than humans. But horses are expensive and often get injured.

They need stables in winter and grass or hay all year round. These are scarce in Japan, especially in mountain regions. Even worse, falls from horseback, in training as well as in battle, can be dangerous. So think carefully! If you could be a samurai, would you really be happy on a horse?

The Ideal Warhorse...

... IS NOT TOO BIG—so you can mount and dismount quickly.

... IS VERY FAST— to carry you away from danger.

Handy Hint

Be thankful that Japan's old enemies—Mongol warriors—invented stirrups. Without them, you might fall off your horse in battle!

Training on Horseback

DURING YOUR TRAINING, you'd be asked to practice shooting arrows while riding at a full gallop. Sometimes the target is made of wood or straw, but sometimes it's a live dog!

Yikes!

Stop right there!

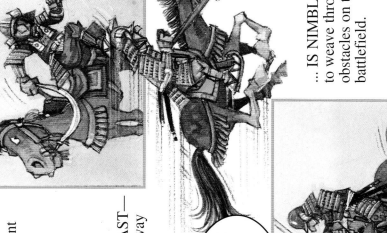

Now that's what I call a high horse!

... IS NIMBLE— to weave through obstacles on the battlefield.

... IS STRONG— to carry you, your armor, and all your weapons.

... IS OBEDIENT— if not, you face disaster!

Could You Be Loyal to a Lord?

ight now, in the early 1600s, Japan is at peace. But from 1185 to 1590, Japan was torn apart by bloody civil wars, with fighting led by various *daimyo* (lords). Most lords were heads of noble families, but some began life as samurai. Each lord controlled a vast area of land and ruled it like a private kingdom. Lords had their own armies, made up of loyal samurai.

There are still many great, rich lords in Japan, and they still need samurai to serve them. To join a lord's army, samurai have to swear undying loyalty and vow to obey without question. Could you ever make such powerful promises?

From Samurai to Warlord

MANY OF TODAY'S great families first gained their power through war. Starting as young samurai from poor but noble families, they won fame and riches by conquering land and capturing enemy castles. Now they rank as daimyo and are proud and powerful.

The warlords' grand castles symbolize their power.

Private samurai armies guard lords and their property.

Farmers pay taxes and rent by giving food to their lords.

Handy Hint

If you really want to fight, join a warlord's army as an ordinary soldier. You might become a samurai's trusted helper.

The Greatest Warlord of All

SHOGUN TOKUGAWA IEYASU, who lived from 1542 to 1616, was the mightiest warlord of recent times—and perhaps the greatest warlord ever. He defeated rivals in 1603 and took control of the Japanese government. He passed strict new laws to end centuries of fighting between rival daimyo and their samurai armies.

My family, the Tokugawa, will rule Japan until 1867!

Wives from ancient noble families help lords gain political power.

Poor, weak nobles are jealous.

Splendid tombs are lasting memorials.

Looted treasures add to lords' riches.

Family badges, displayed on flags and clothes, are signs of power.

Are You Strong and Self-disciplined?

> The sword, the mind, and the body are one.

Are you healthy and athletic? Lean and trim? Are your muscles tough and brawny? A samurai must keep fit at all times. His body is one of his weapons! Martial-arts training, exercise, and fasting will help him to control his mind and body. So will a moderate lifestyle, ritual baths, and regular prayer and meditation. All of these things will purify him and prepare him to follow *bushido*, the samurai code, also known as "the way of the warrior."

A true samurai must put duty first—ignoring his own hopes and fears, and sometimes even the needs of his family. Do you think you could ever do this— and would you want to?

The Path of Zen

INNER PEACE. Zen is a way of following the Buddhist religion. Zen has been widely taught in Japan since the AD 1200s. It is especially popular with samurai.

Zen teachers, most of whom are monks, encourage their followers to seek enlightenment (spiritual understanding) through meditation, feats of bravery, and endurance.

Handy Hint

As a warrior, you're never off duty! Take this advice from Takeda, a wise samurai: "Keep your sword with you at all times, even when you are alone."

Zen Gardens

STRESSED OUT? If a samurai is finding it tough to obey the bushido code, he takes some time out to meditate in a beautiful, harmonious Zen garden. The soothing surroundings will help free his mind from fears and worries, so that he can find inner strength.

What is the sound of one hand clapping?

Swoosh!

Bushido Demands:

- Honesty
- Bravery
- Skill
- Loyalty
- Self-discipline
- Obedience

Could you make the grade?

Courageous Comrades

Even if you could become a high-ranking, well-trained samurai, you'd be just one among thousands. Before the early 1600s, when the shogun began to force lords to make peace, great daimyo kept private armies of over 100,000 men! Today these armies are smaller, but they are still impressive fighting machines.

In battle, every soldier has a vital part to play. His comrades rely on him to do his duty and be courageous. If he fails, or is cowardly, their lives could be in danger. Battles may sound exciting and glorious, but in reality they are bloody and brutal—and very, very frightening.

Swish!

Swish!

Swipe!

Can't we talk about this?

Handy Hint

To display your brilliance on the battlefield, bring home some heads of slaughtered enemies!

Dangerous Honor

IN BATTLE, samurai and ordinary soldiers rally around *nobori* (banners) bearing their warlord's badge. Being chosen to carry a banner on your back is a great honor—but very dangerous, since you become an easy target!

Show some respect!

Who called my mother a donkey?!

AS A SAMURAI SWORDSMAN on horseback, you'd charge toward the enemy alongside troops trained in many other fighting skills: archers, spear-throwers, gunmen, and foot soldiers armed with heavy wooden sticks or long, deadly knives.

Could You Live For Weeks in the Wild?

A re you a homebody? Do you like to be warm and cozy? If you were a samurai, you'd be away from home for weeks, months, or even years. You'd be out on patrol, guarding your lord's land, or you'd be advancing into enemy territory. You'd sleep on the ground, climb mountains, face snow in winter and heavy rain in summer, and have little food. To top it off, you'd be at constant risk of an enemy attack!

Did anyone else hear that?

Shhh!

The "Joys" of Military Life:

Handy Hint

Did you bring a cooking pot for cooking water and boiling dinner? cooking dinner?— Probably not— they're heavy and they're fragile. Use your helmet instead!

Telltale Signs

HOW DO you know if an enemy is approaching? You could send scouts to look for them—but they might be caught and killed. You could ask local people—but they might betray you. It would be safer to keep a lookout for telltale signs, such as smoke from campfires or birds disturbed by the marching enemy, squawking and flapping in the distance.

HEAVY GOING. You'd be weighed down by weapons, food rations, and your sleeping mat.

SCARY STUFF. At night, strange noises would keep you awake—are they signs of danger?

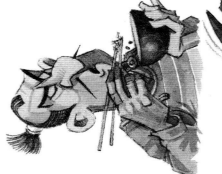

JUST A SCRATCH. Your armor—which is worn all the time—might get infested by lice.

I want my mom!

Hoo!

BORING MEALS. Every day, your meals would be the same—boiled rice and (if you're lucky) dried tuna.

DESPERATE TIMES. If you ran out of rations, you'd have to catch wild animals to survive!

Could You Storm an Enemy's Castle?

For the past 100 years, great lords have built magnificent castles in many parts of Japan. These castles are homes for themselves and their families, barracks for their samurai soldiers, and offices for the staff who manage their lands.

And of course, they are mighty fortresses to keep out invaders. In 1600, Shogun Tokugawa Ieyasu seized 87 castles in the richest parts of Japan and banished their owners to remote regions, where he hoped they could do no harm. Now, some of these lords want to send samurai to recapture their castles. This will not be easy—each building was specially designed to withstand attacks.

Defensive Devices

1. Ramparts (outer defensive barriers)
2. Deep moats
3. High outer walls
4. Steep, sloping stone bases
5. Smooth, sheer walls of the central keep (the main fortress)
6. Watchtowers for lookouts
7. Small, narrow windows

Handy Hint

If you can't climb into a castle, use fire! Castles' inner walls are built of wood and plaster and burn very quickly.

Prince Yamato

ONE FAMOUS STORY tells how legendary samurai Prince Yamato (see page 11) disguised himself as an old woman to trick the samurai guarding an enemy castle. With traditional Japanese respect for old age, the guards graciously invited "her" to enter!

No problem, granny.

Ooh, what a helpful young man you are!

5

6

7

Do You Love Honor More than Life?

Just suppose you could achieve your dream, and became a samurai. Could you maintain the high standards of behavior that everyone would expect from you? Your family, your lord, your comrades, and your friends would all take pride in your fighting skills. They would share your joys and triumphs, but how would you—and they—feel if you failed?

THESE THINGS would bring shame on you and your family:

Running away in battle

Aaah!

I heard my daimyo keeps his gold in his....

Betraying your lord for money or power

Making foolish decisions that lead to defeat in battle

One of the worst things a samurai can do is bring shame to his friends and loved ones. If a samurai murders, cheats, lies, steals, betrays comrades, or lets himself get captured, he might be tempted to choose death rather than dishonor. But listen carefully—harming yourself is never, ever the right thing to do! Always remember that it's much better to stay alive and learn from your failures. Just try not to make the same mistakes again.

Handy Hint

Try to lead a good, honest life! That way, you'll be remembered and honored with a fancy tomb when you die.

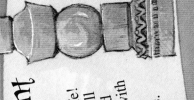

Try to Stay Alive!

JAPANESE DOCTORS do their best to heal injured samurai. But if there's no doctor nearby, try *kanpo* (traditional remedies), such as bathing wounds with heated urine, or eating horse-dung mixed with water to stop bleeding!

Whose idea was this?

Being responsible for a comrade's death

Stealing, lying, cheating, or committing some other crime

Getting captured by enemies

The Myth of Minamoto no Tametomo

SAMURAI Minamoto no Tametomo was said to have killed himself rather than face defeat. But it's also said that he won 20 battles in just two years, and that one of his arms was magically longer than the other! Are any of these stories really true?

The Last Samurai?

ou'll find this hard to believe, but several hundred years from now, there will be no more samurai in Japan. If you could travel into the future, you'd find that laws passed by the Tokugawa family—the shoguns who rule Japan—mean that samurai warriors are no longer needed.

Under these new laws, there is peace at home in Japan, and very little contact with foreigners. Samurai will keep their rank and their traditions but will no longer be warriors. In 1867, there will be a revolution and the last Tokugawa shogun will be overthrown. New Japanese industries will develop—and samurai will be history!

The future lies with industry and business, not old-fashioned samurai.

But the samurai way should not be forgotten.

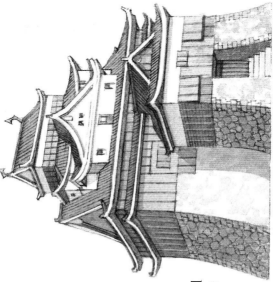

Handy Hint

Study martial arts and take part in a living tradition. Kendo, judo, and karate are all based on samurai skills.

Their Fame Will Live Forever!

IN THEIR DREAMS, kids today can still join a samurai army and share in their glorious adventures. Millions of children around the world are fascinated by samurai.

HONORABLE MEMORY. Samurai bravery, loyalty, and noble self-sacrifice will inspire soldiers, sailors, and fighter pilots for centuries.

PROUD HERITAGE. Some samurai castles will be carefully preserved, so that everyone can marvel at their strength and beauty.

ON DISPLAY. Samurai weapons and armor will be displayed in museums, for visitors to study and admire.

MEDIA HEROES. Samurai warriors will star in epic adventures in films, computer games, and *manga* cartoon books.

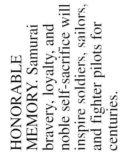

Glossary

Ashigaru An ordinary soldier in a Japanese warlord's army; an ashigaru is lower-ranking than a samurai.

Buddhist Someone who follows the teachings of the spiritual leader known as the Buddha (the Enlightened One), who lived in India around 550 BC. The Buddha taught his followers to work to end suffering by living thoughtful, honest, and peaceful lives.

Bushido Rules for good behavior that samurai were meant to follow. Also known as "the way of the warrior."

Chain mail Flexible armor made by joining hundreds of small metal rings together.

Daimyo A lord who owned large estates and was the head of a noble family. Often, a daimyo also led his own samurai army.

Enlightenment Spiritual truth and understanding.

Genbuku A ceremony at the end of samurai training to mark the time when a teenage boy became a man and a warrior.

Go An ancient board game. As in chess, winning is based on intelligence and strategy (careful planning).

Kanpo Traditional Japanese medicine.

Katana A long, curved sword, worn with the sharp edge of the blade facing up.

Keep The central fortress of a castle.

Manga Brightly illustrated comic books that sometimes feature samurai heroes. They are very popular in modern Japan.

Martial arts Combat sports based on warriors' fighting techniques. They include judo (unarmed contests using balance and self-control), karate (contests using the hands and other parts of the body), and kendo (contests using wooden or bamboo swords).

Meditation A spiritual practice that involves sitting quietly for a long period of time.

Moderate Mild and calm—not extreme.

Mongols An East Asian people famous for their fighting skills. They ruled a large empire stretching from China to the Black Sea in the 1200s.

Nobori Banners carried by warriors, usually decorated with the badge of their lord or battle commander.

Ramparts The defensive walls of a castle.

Rawhide The tough, untreated skin of an animal.

Samurai Meaning "men who serve," these were expert warriors who fought in armies led by great Japanese lords.

Shogun Meaning "great general," this was the most senior soldier in Japan, who led national armies on behalf of the emperor. From 1185 to 1867,

shoguns were essentially the rulers of Japan.

Surcoat A tunic or cloak made of cloth, sometimes worn to cover samurai armor. The back was often decorated with a the badge of a samurai's lord or battle commander.

Tsuba A circular or oval guard fitted next to the handle of a sword to protect one's fingers from the sharp blade.

Zen A way of following the Buddhist faith that was popular among samurai soldiers. Zen encourages meditation, self-discipline, and endurance.

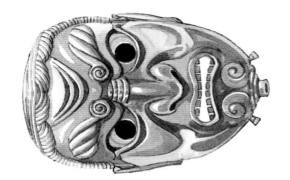

Index